First Edition published in Canada in 2020

Text, Artwork, Layout and production Michael.R.Harris P.Eng
Printed and bound in the United States by Lightning Source Inc

Artistic production work for this book was done using Coreldraw and Microsoft Word on an Apple iMac.

Library Filing Information

ISBN 978-1-7771863-0-2

Canadian Poetry
Harris, Michael R. 1942 -
Sunshine Beckons: Poems and Illustrations/Michael R Harris

This work is partly autobiographical
with considerable artistic licence.
It was inspired by Teva Harrison,
who I wish I had known.
Her little book
"Not one of these poems is about you"
touched me by it's complete honesty
and immense courage.

Michael R Harris

For Judith

CONTENTS

to remember is
to love
to love is
to remember
let the flood gates
of memory open
and a warm wave
sweep me
away to where
I'll never forget
I know one day
they must go
these gifts
my sight, my ear
take them away
one by one
but as long
as I'm alive
as long
as I can love
please
make my memories
last to go

boyhood memories
CHAPTER ONE
Killbull Box Co.

sunshine beckons little flower
show your face to me
come on out don' t be afraid
the audience murmurs
the stage is set
you have a life to play
I'll see you after the ovation

on my mother's lap
after falling down stairs
all those hugs and kisses

I know for sure she cares.

the chimney on our house
it moans and wails at night
dad says
not to worry, just the wind

but it gives me a fright

the chimney got a cowl
the ghost has gone – hooray
trouble is now

it whistles during the day

a piece by verdi
not likely

unless rendered
by a chorus of sparrows

dad says we'll be moving soon anyway
give me more room to play

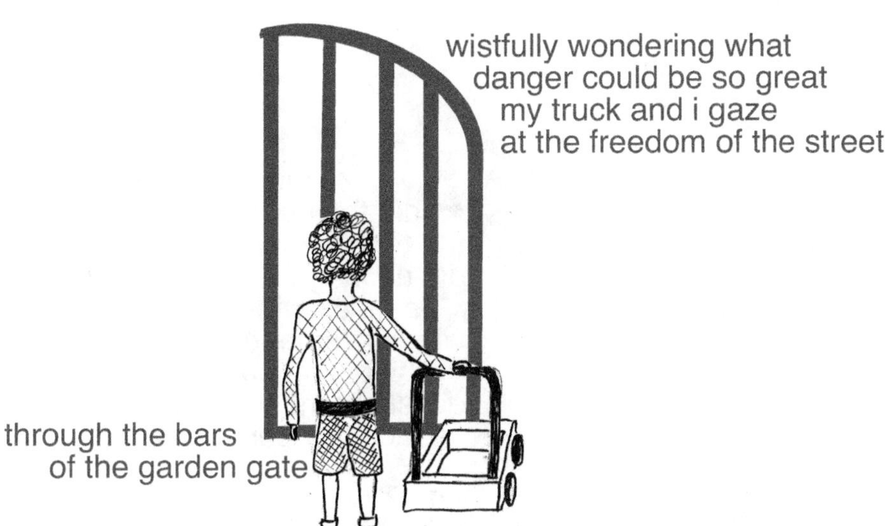

wistfully wondering what
danger could be so great
my truck and i gaze
at the freedom of the street

through the bars
of the garden gate

being myself
but small
it hurts when I'm ignored

hey it's me - I'm here

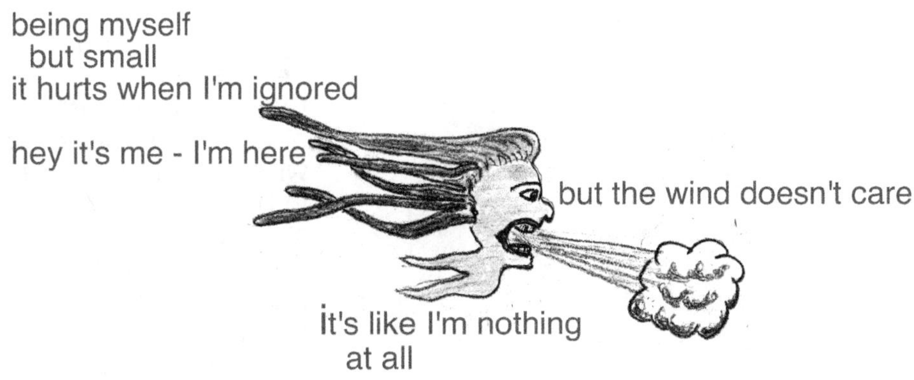

but the wind doesn't care

it's like I'm nothing
at all

in my stroller
I thought it was fun
when my mother
began to run
but soon
I sensed the fear
as the roar
of the aircraft drew near
did the german pilot know
the terror created below
did he laugh a mirthless laugh
as he exacted Hitler's wrath
with his finger on the trigger
why did he pause
did st peters shadow
suddenly seem bigger

he died
my first
experience of grief
loss
one of the family
gone

sooty, our cat

by his name you know
he wasn't red
that was the color
of our neighbours face
when she found him
in her flower bed
she would throw
buckets of water
never hit him
not once
till he got old and sick
good old sooty
what's a poor cat to do

there was no ritual
to come to terms with the death
to mourn
cats don't rank that high
except in our hearts

it's o.k. you'll be alright

what place is this
crowds of strangers
in strange rooms
doing strange things

here; here; here; here
forty times here

ran all the way home

how was your first day of school
didn't know what to say
it was o.k.

now I get a teacher
born of satan I wonder
refused to be excused

my disgrace
no accidental blunder

every Christmas the journey north
we'd stay with Auntie Phyl
mum's hot celery soup it was
that warmed that winter chill
from riding pillion on dad's bike
with sidecar
little bro' and mother safe inside

I can taste it still

I am so excited
I can hardly sit still
Christmas with my cousins
an annual thrill
Will Santa Claus come

I bet he will

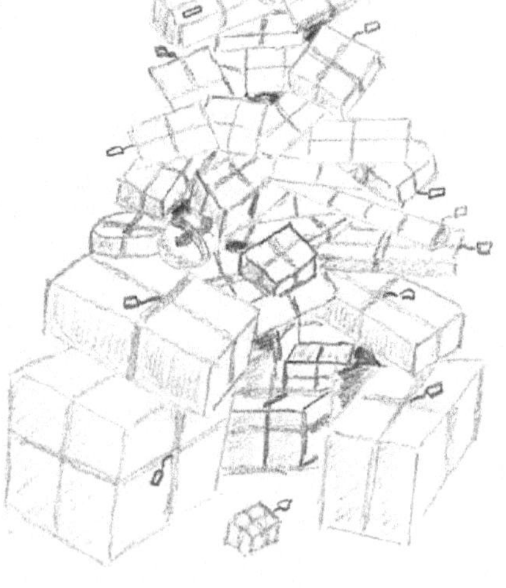

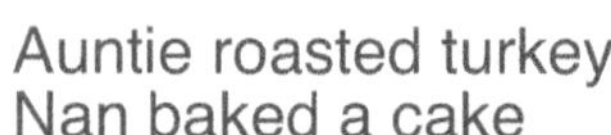

Auntie roasted turkey
Nan baked a cake

and there was so much to eat
it made my stomach ache

auntie had a toby jug
stood upon the mantle
played a pretty tune
when lifted by the handle
my mother would go ape
when she heard that pretty tune
as her boy stood on tip toe
to hear the old man croon

free and wild
bike and road
place to be

so long as I'm home
in time for tea

the woods and the downs
the beach and the rocks
place for a boy to grow

alone by choice
as puberty knocks

14

a storm on the chalk cliffs
waves crashing
on the black rocks below
a seagull wheels and screams
a small figure stands
on the edge
entranced

his beating heart dreams

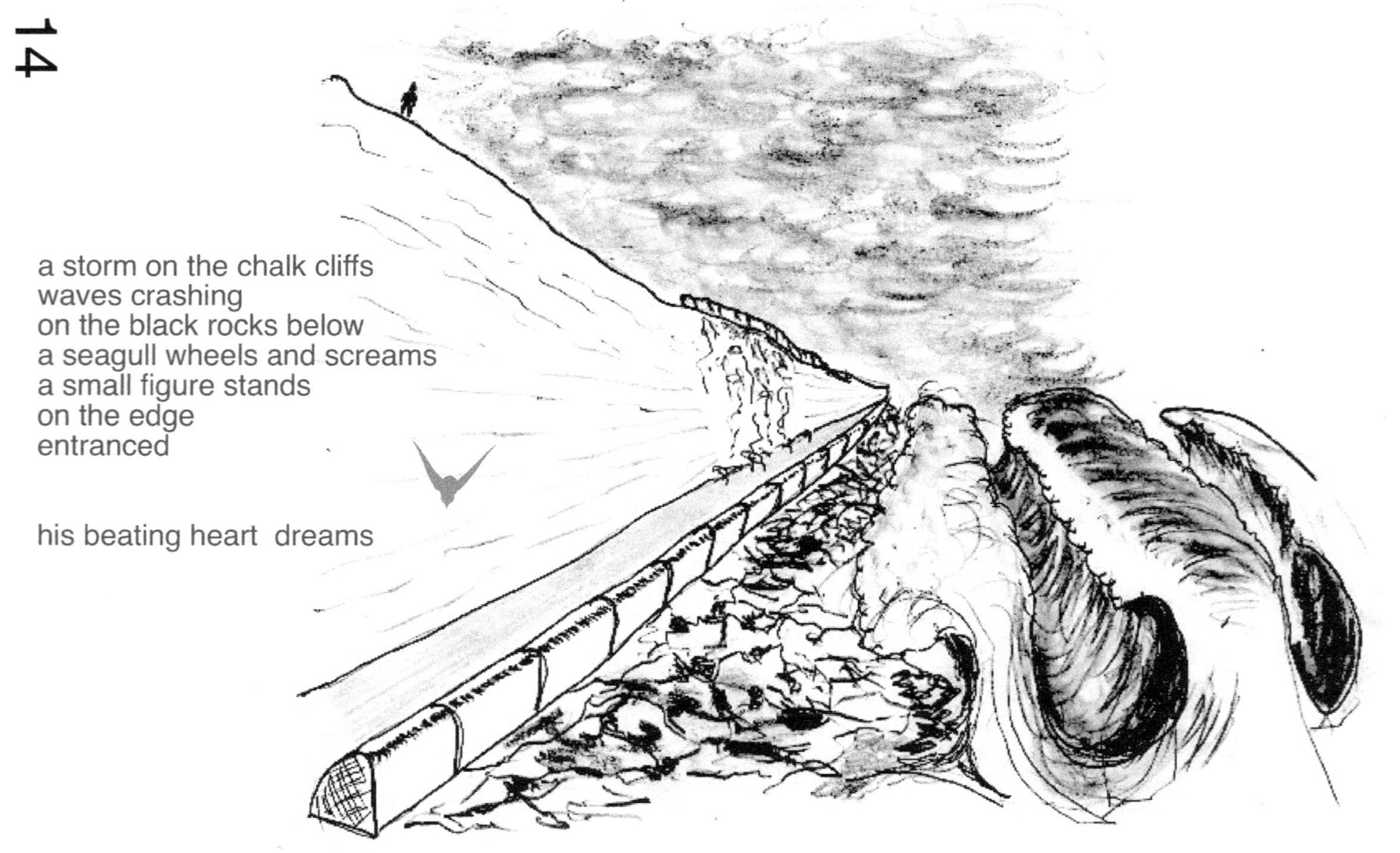

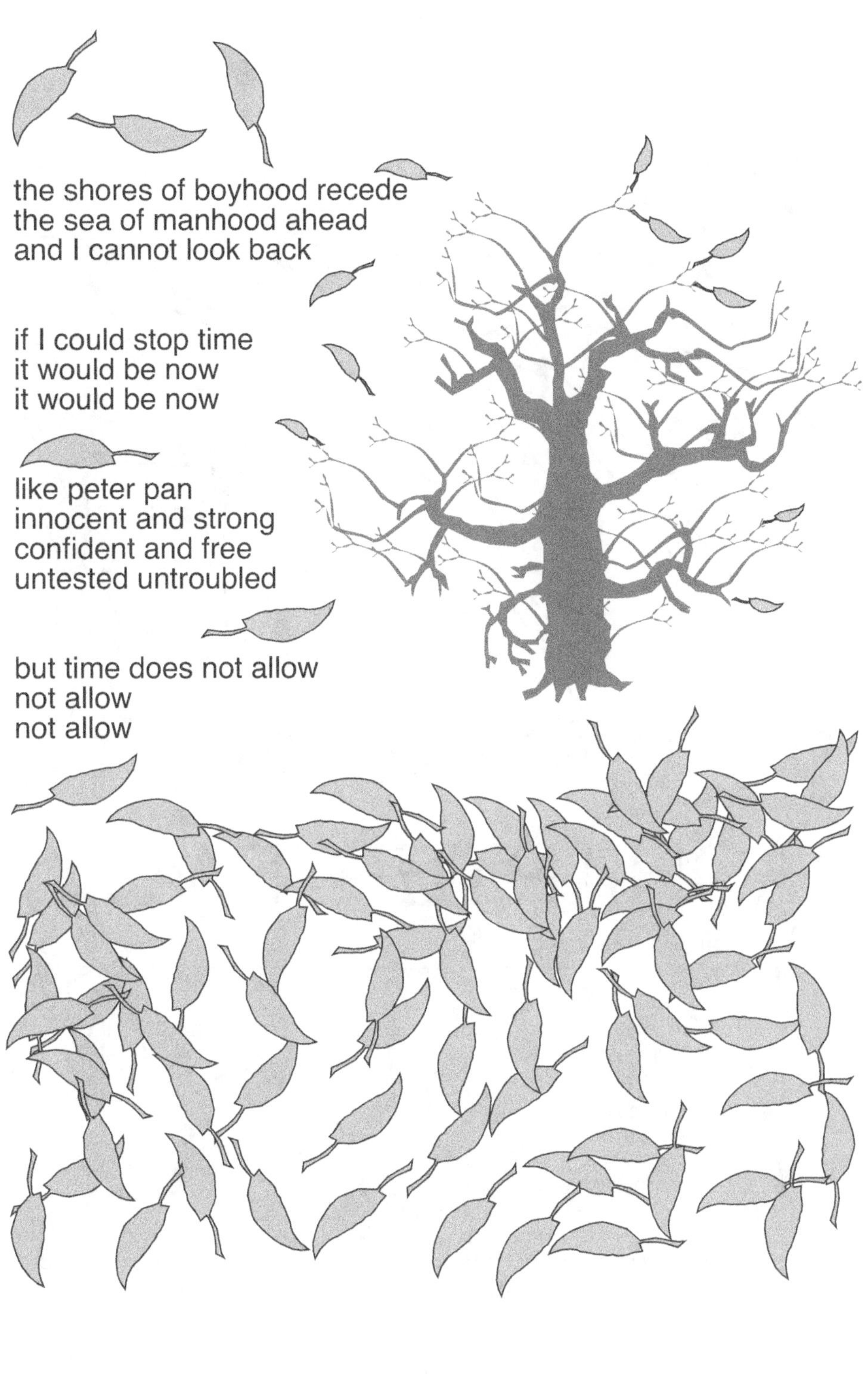

the shores of boyhood recede
the sea of manhood ahead
and I cannot look back

if I could stop time
it would be now
it would be now

like peter pan
innocent and strong
confident and free
untested untroubled

but time does not allow
not allow
not allow

memories of youth
CHAPTER TWO
Killbull Box Co.

high school friends a few
bent on adventure and dare
each outdoing the other
faint of heart beware
be careful where you step
along the electric rail
one false move
and more than
you know
will fail

take the boys camping
a midnight hike
and no-one will tell

if they do something we like

the roar of the waves
as they hit the beach
the suck at the pebbles
as it breaths in again

and I'm in
sounds muffled and mixed
sights blue green
till I gasp at the surface
to dive even deeper

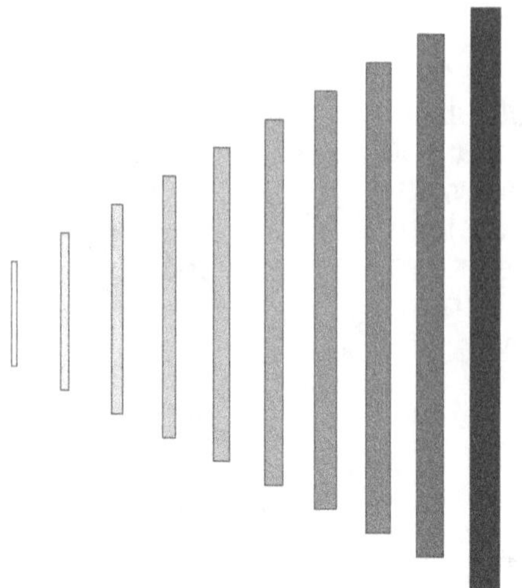

walking
in fog
“NO ENTRY” sign
way back
familiar sights
fewer and fewer
on this journey
I'm lost

yet somehow not

life is overwhelming
so in bravado I hide
reaching out for friends
but in my armor I can't be touched

the wind at my back
the rain in my face
more like flying than running

easy pace
easy pace
easy pace

testosterone, talcum and sweat
the dojo
shuffling feet and shouts
bodies thump on mat
feelings
as old as judo itself

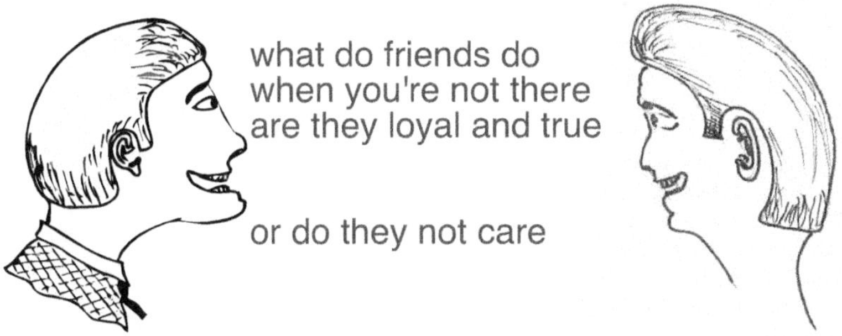

what do friends do
when you're not there
are they loyal and true

or do they not care

some days good some days not
I do my very best
success is sometimes easy

to heck with the rest

women are a mystery
understand them if you can
they amuse and bemuse

for I'm just an ordinary man

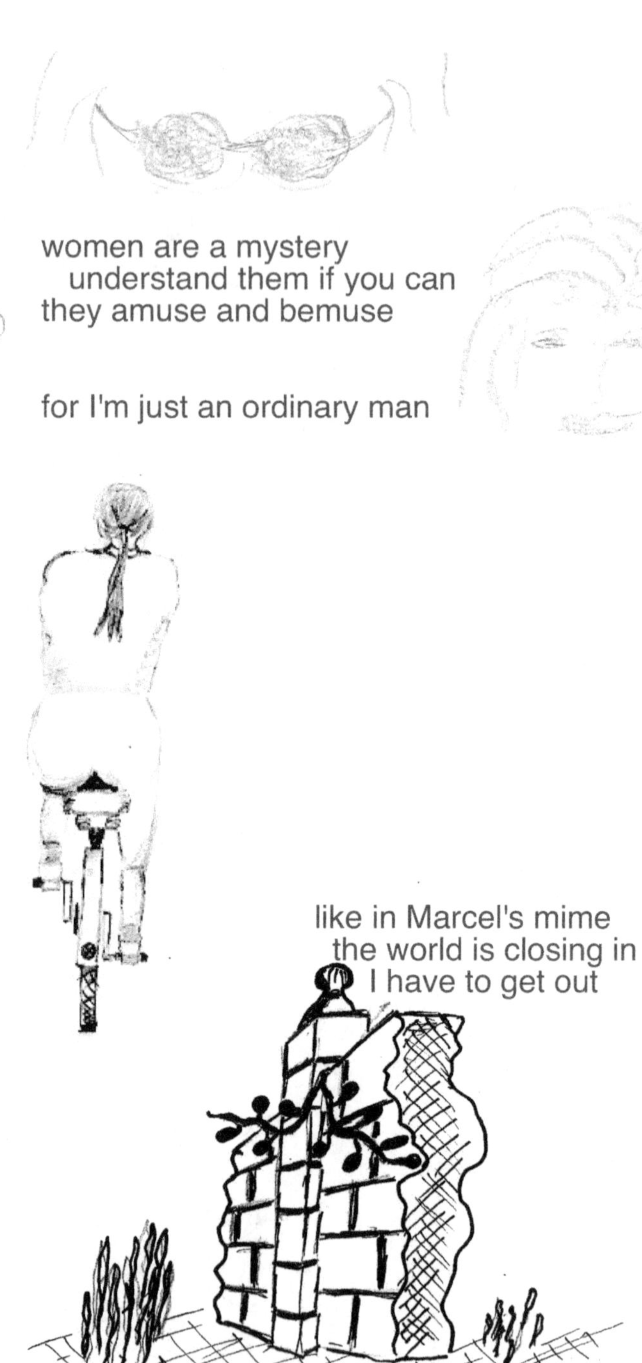

like in Marcel's mime
the world is closing in
I have to get out

and go where I can grow.

young man's memories
CHAPTER THREE
Killbull Box Co.

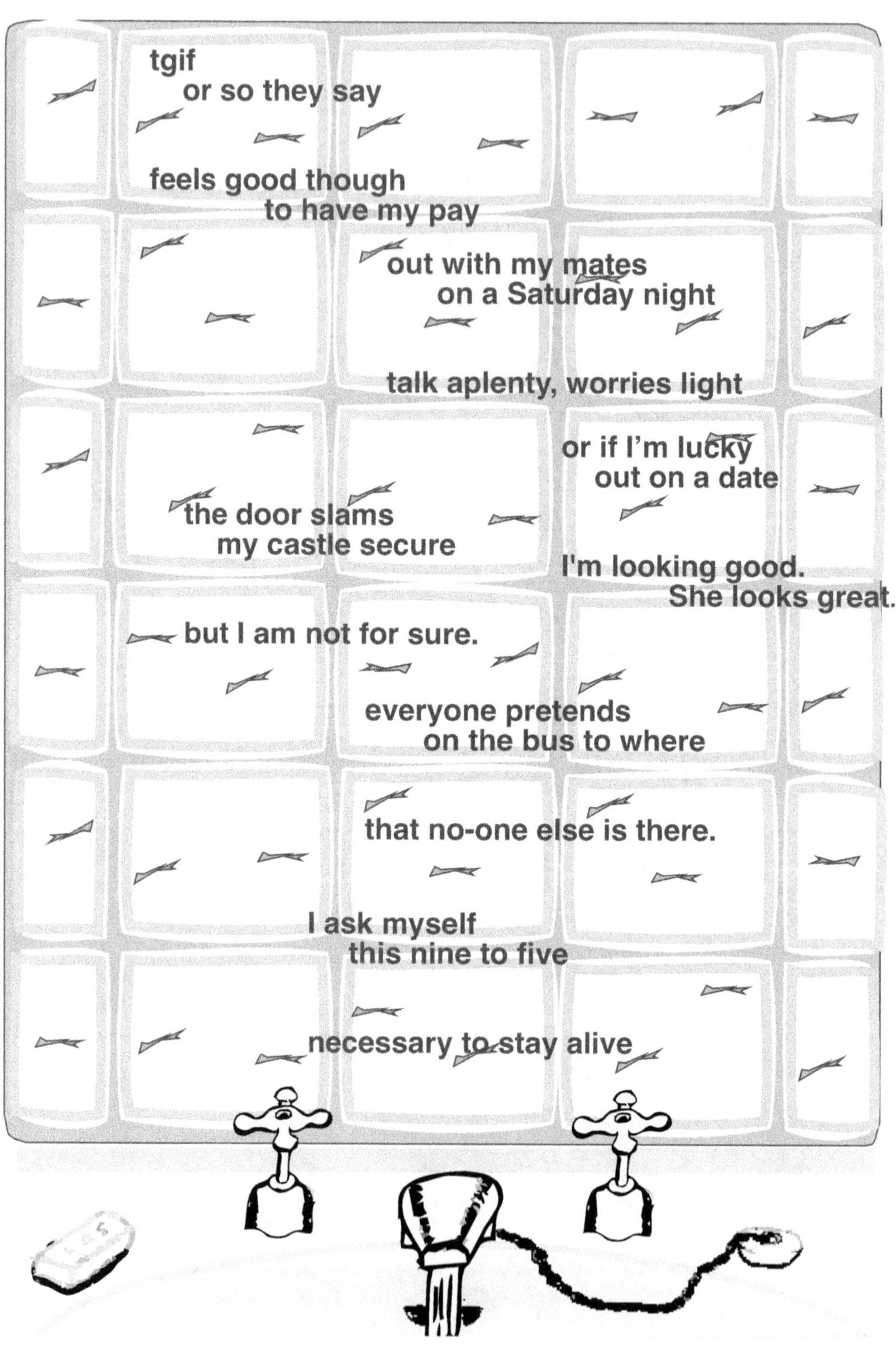
tgif
or so they say
feels good though
to have my pay
out with my mates
on a Saturday night
talk aplenty, worries light
or if I'm lucky
out on a date
the door slams
my castle secure
I'm looking good.
She looks great.
but I am not for sure.
everyone pretends
on the bus to where
that no-one else is there.
I ask myself
this nine to five
necessary to stay alive

I dreamt I was wrong
that’s right I was wrong
was the dream wrong
or if it was right
then did it really happen
could the dream be
right and I was wrong
or am I wrong
about that
It was only a dream
afterall

work, work, work
and do what 'ere I can
so I can stand up straight
and owe not any man
,,,,,,,,,,,,er
'cept the credit union
yes them ....er and the bank
ooh! and the credit card company
don't forget the the car loan
then there's the tax man
oh! and the ....
work, work, work.

ahoy, oh joy, oh love
a baby boy
his little hand in mine
to remind me
of my humanity
which almost got forgotten
somewhere
along the line

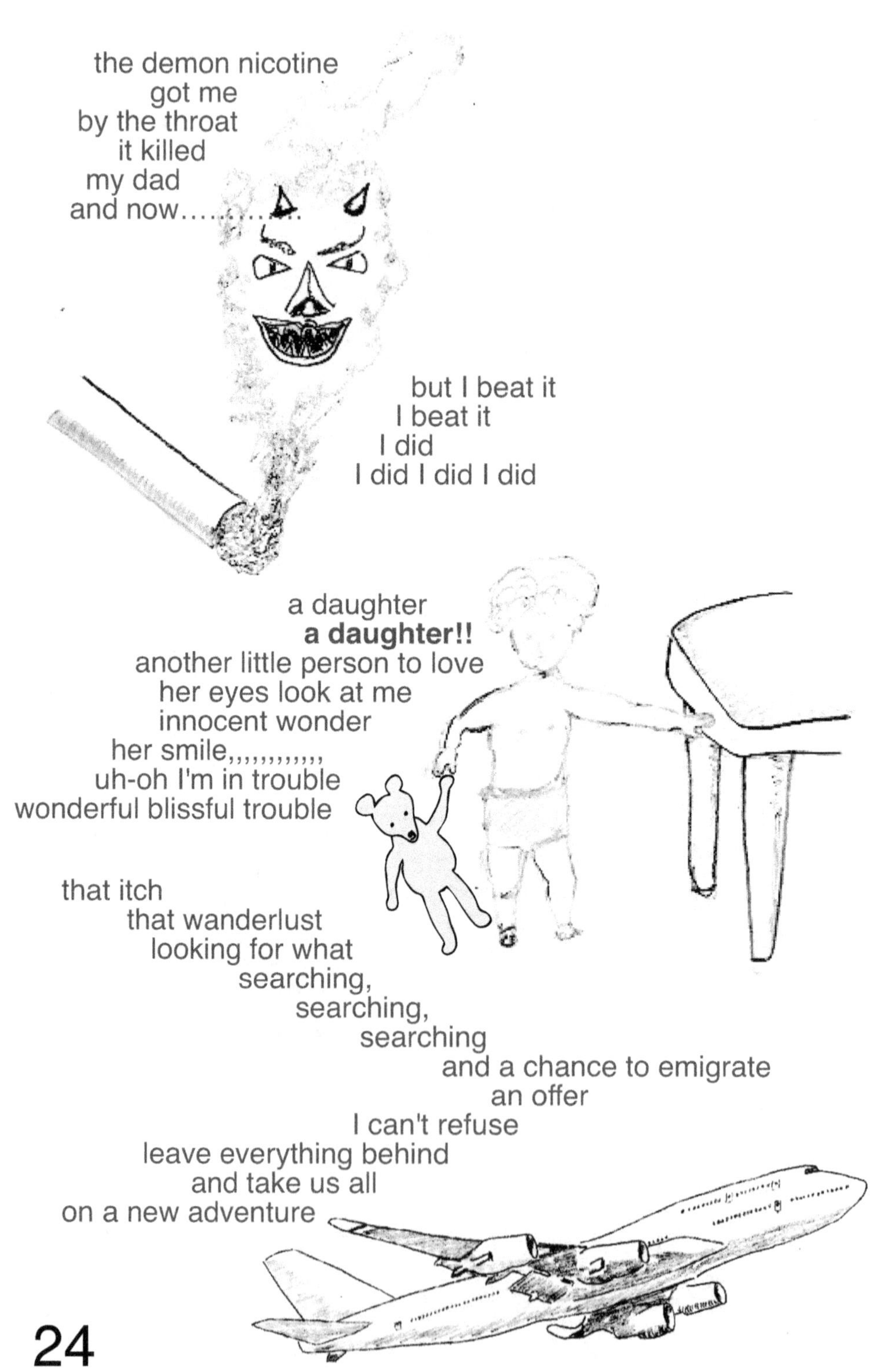

the demon nicotine
got me
by the throat
it killed
my dad
and now…………

but I beat it
I beat it
I did
I did I did I did

a daughter
a daughter!!
another little person to love
her eyes look at me
innocent wonder
her smile,,,,,,,,,,,
uh-oh I'm in trouble
wonderful blissful trouble

that itch
that wanderlust
looking for what
searching,
searching,
searching
and a chance to emigrate
an offer
I can't refuse
leave everything behind
and take us all
on a new adventure

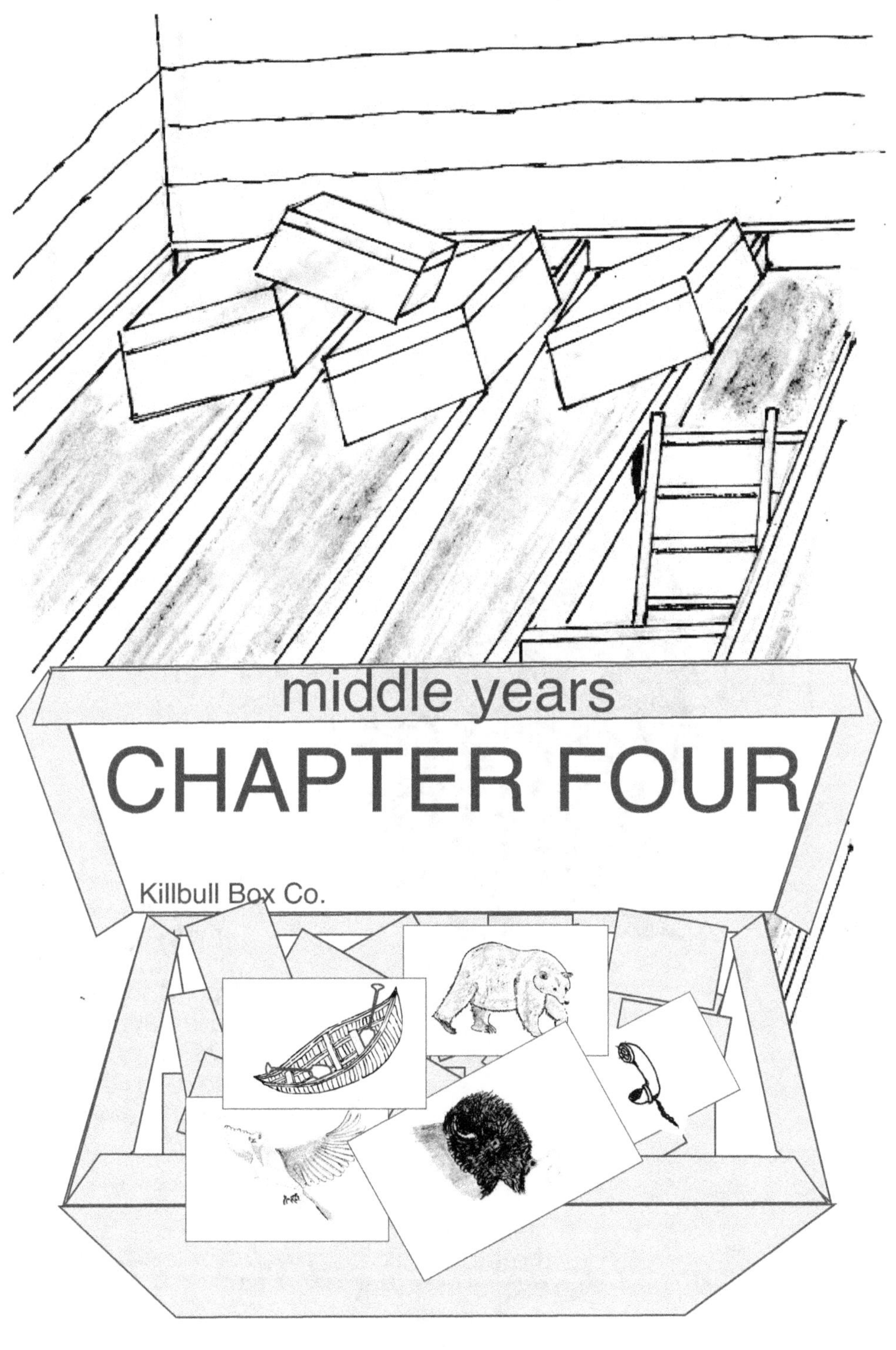
middle years
CHAPTER FOUR
Killbull Box Co.

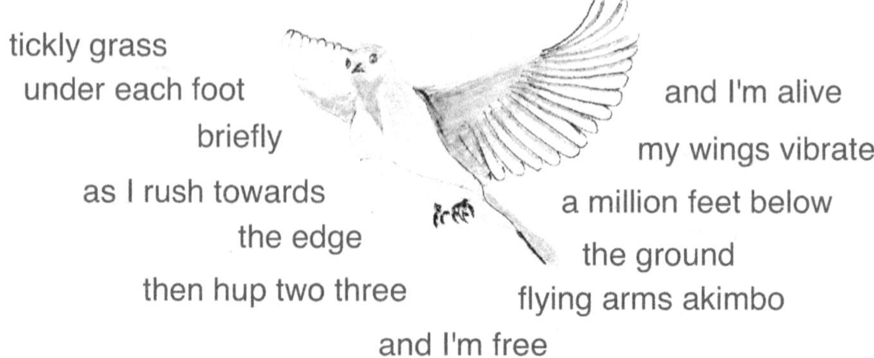

tickly grass
under each foot
briefly
as I rush towards
the edge
then hup two three
flying arms akimbo
and I'm alive
my wings vibrate
a million feet below
the ground
and I'm free

in elk island park
with new eyes
I see
the old
and not so old
they move
on the road
as one body
the bison
they rock
the car
side to side
tires squeal
we are chaff
in their wind
or another bison
something wrong
with him
they don't know
we are immigrants
forgive us
and now
they are gone
moved on
and our fear
prevented us
from enjoying
the moment
a unique moment
a rare intimacy
with the wild.

forty below
seven foot of snow
roots and shoots
under
dream of spring

to go
or not
the power
the control
the road
old friend
wheel in my hands
    ornament on the hood
and after all this time
    still feels good

actual conversation
        Hello
Hello this is Mick
        Can I get your last name Nick
no Mick
        yes Nick
no Mick m-i-c-k
        yes Nick n-i-c-k
no m as in mother
        n as in nother?
how about Michael.
        what about Michael
I'll call back. Bye.

the badlands
so called
fossils huge
dinosaur ghosts
wander
a roar
down a canyon
and earth trembles
hoodoo memories

she smiles
she's happy
heart open wide
so how did this happen
after the years
I need to hide

tiny little bird
so free to fly
wish I were you
up in the sky
I would go to Paris
or Zanzibar or Rome
if I were free to fly
I'd rarely be home

light growing dim
dark during day
nothing I can do
nothing you can say

save me oh save me
keep me in bliss
tremble oh tremble
near the abyss

I swim in it's fragrance
a flower p'r'aps a rose
and it lifts my heart up
up, up, up, up to
heaven knows.

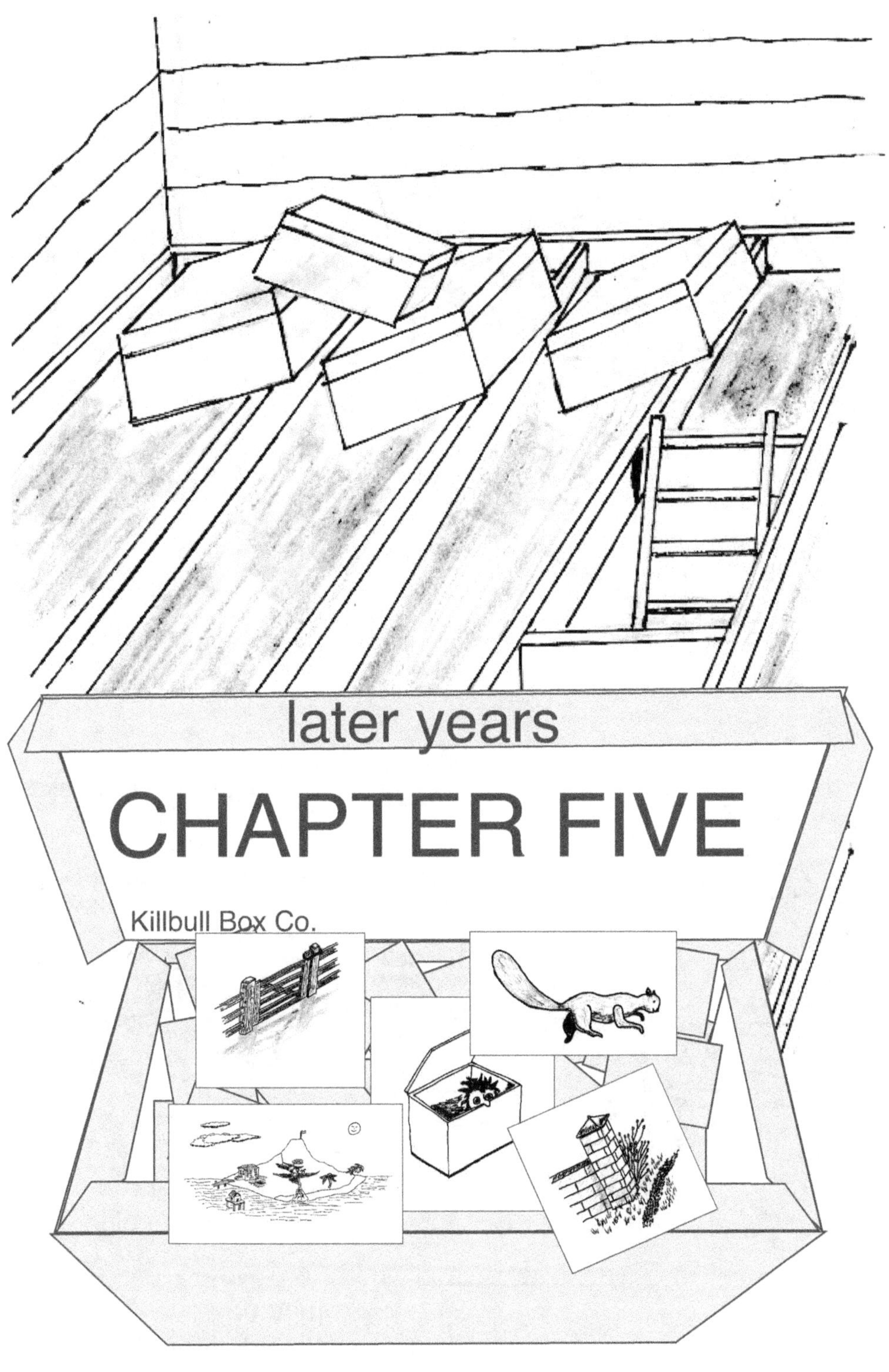
later years
CHAPTER FIVE
Killbull Box Co.

it seems I have a soul
it came out quite unbidden
how very inconvenient

get back to where you w're hidden

to love again
to jump in that lake

carefulness, tenderness
serenely I quake

an emerald isle
in the blue

good or
too good to be true

a silhouette chugs
along the horizon
bound for
places unknown
across blue-green
and calm
glitter in the sun
as far as eye can see
the beach smells salty
with ancient hints
but wavelets suck
at my toes
I'm harmless
they would say
come on
it's o.k.

tho' built up now
trees to the mill
the sounds of the forest
they resonate still
the smell of the dankwood
hangs on the hill
and a little boy's heart
roams at will

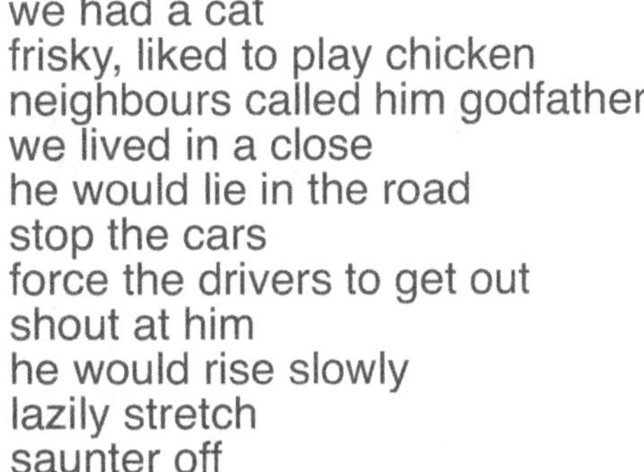

we had a cat
frisky, liked to play chicken
neighbours called him godfather
we lived in a close
he would lie in the road
stop the cars
force the drivers to get out
shout at him
he would rise slowly
lazily stretch
saunter off

dangerous?
you would think
but he knew which cars
would stop
if he saw one coming
that he knew wouldn't
he got out of the way p.d.q

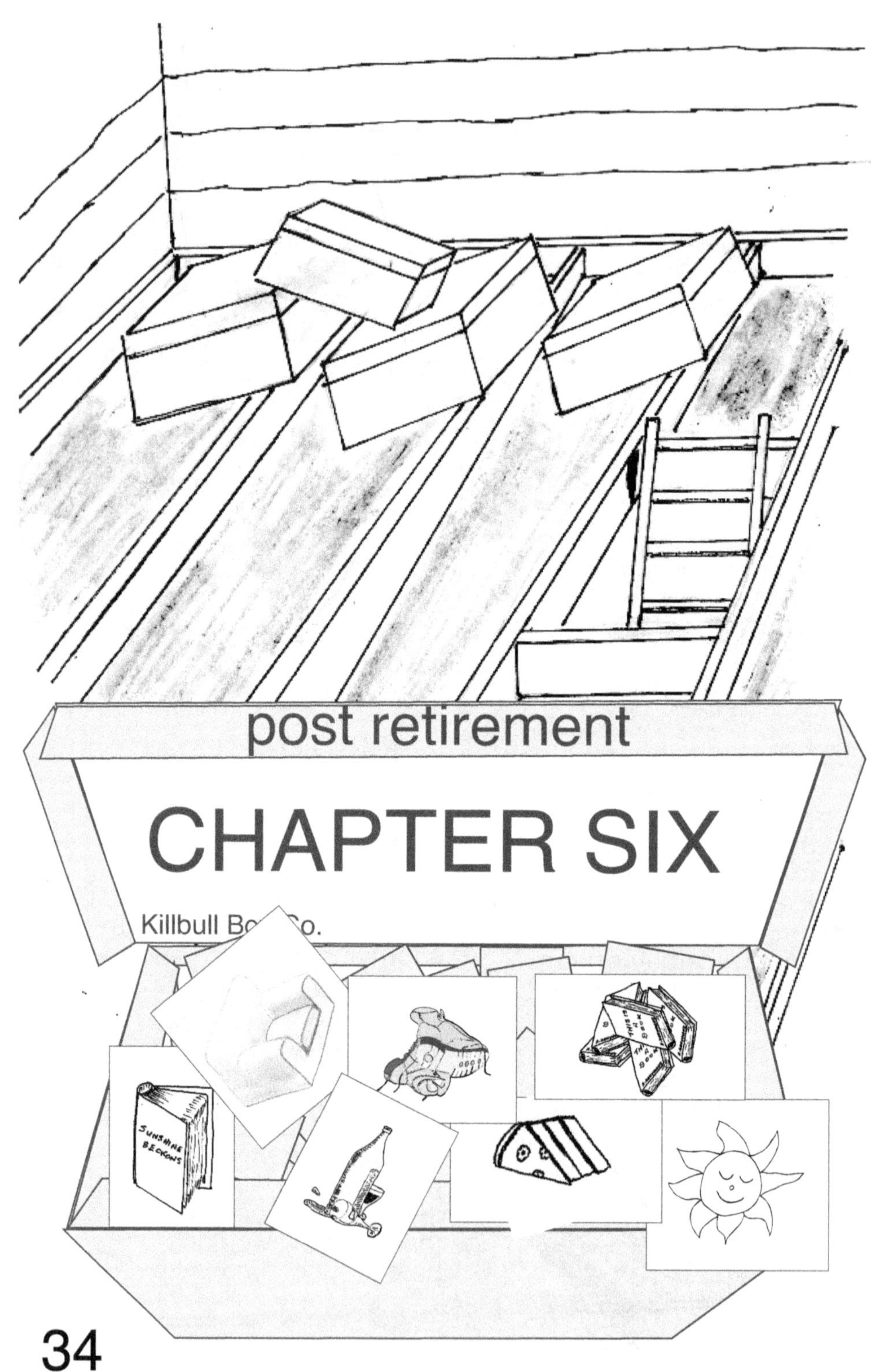
post retirement
CHAPTER SIX
Killbull Bo Co.
SUNSHINE BECKONS

there's something i must do
I'll remember if I think
I don't know what it is

but I will in just a wink

the sunshine is
making it too hot
in my cozy bed

I see a new mum
I see a new dad
it makes my heart sing

it makes my heart glad.

is it up to some trick
trying to mess
with my head.

looking after grandkids
in the park
rough house play
trouble was
couldn't get up
next day

the clouds are pretty today
glowing rosy
as they catch the sun
I suppose

it must be dark below
but I don't care about that
not today
I'm above it all

retiring was easy
being retired is not
well not as easy as claimed
what was I saying
- I forgot
I hurt
all over
a little bit
like I've been beaten
by tiny men
with baseball bats
and in some places
a bit more
some places
even have places
I didn't used
to hurt
even whisky
doesn't work so well
brief moments of relief
in a hot bath
just before sleep
and stubbing my toe
which takes my mind
of all the other places
the alarm goes off
at six, up, dressed
and out
in the office at seven
eat lunch at my desk
get back home
not much before seven
monday to friday
the working week
saturdays sometimes too
oh thank heaven
it's just a distant memory
I still go to work but
in different fashion
now I go to work
to follow my passion

food is good
better than sex
for several reasons

it can last
as long as you like
for a man anyway

if things don't go well
you can always blame the chef

there are a thousand varieties of sex but
there are a million varieties of food

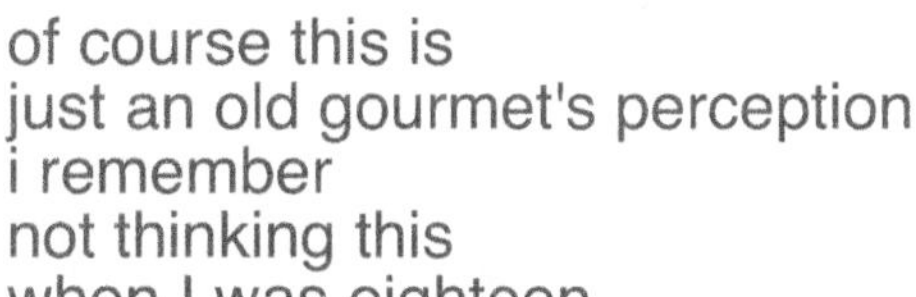

of course this is
just an old gourmet's perception
i remember
not thinking this
when I was eighteen.

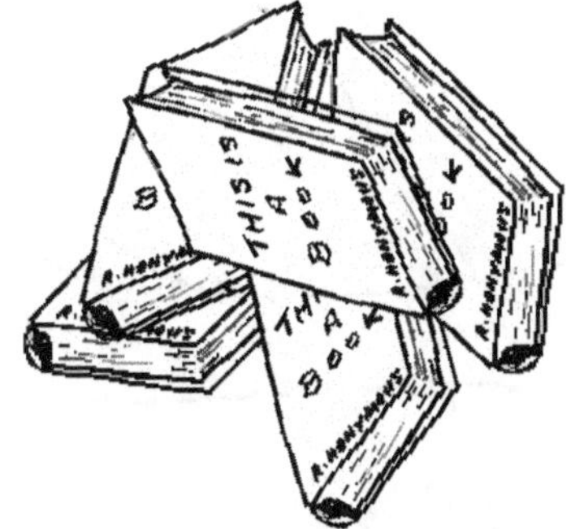

book clubs are great
and reading books is fun
and most members are good

but seems there's always one
book I mean
always one book

I'll write my biography
something to be read
by no-one and nobody

after i'm dead

pople you vaguely remember
like ghosts in the mist
each offers a gentle wave
turns slowly

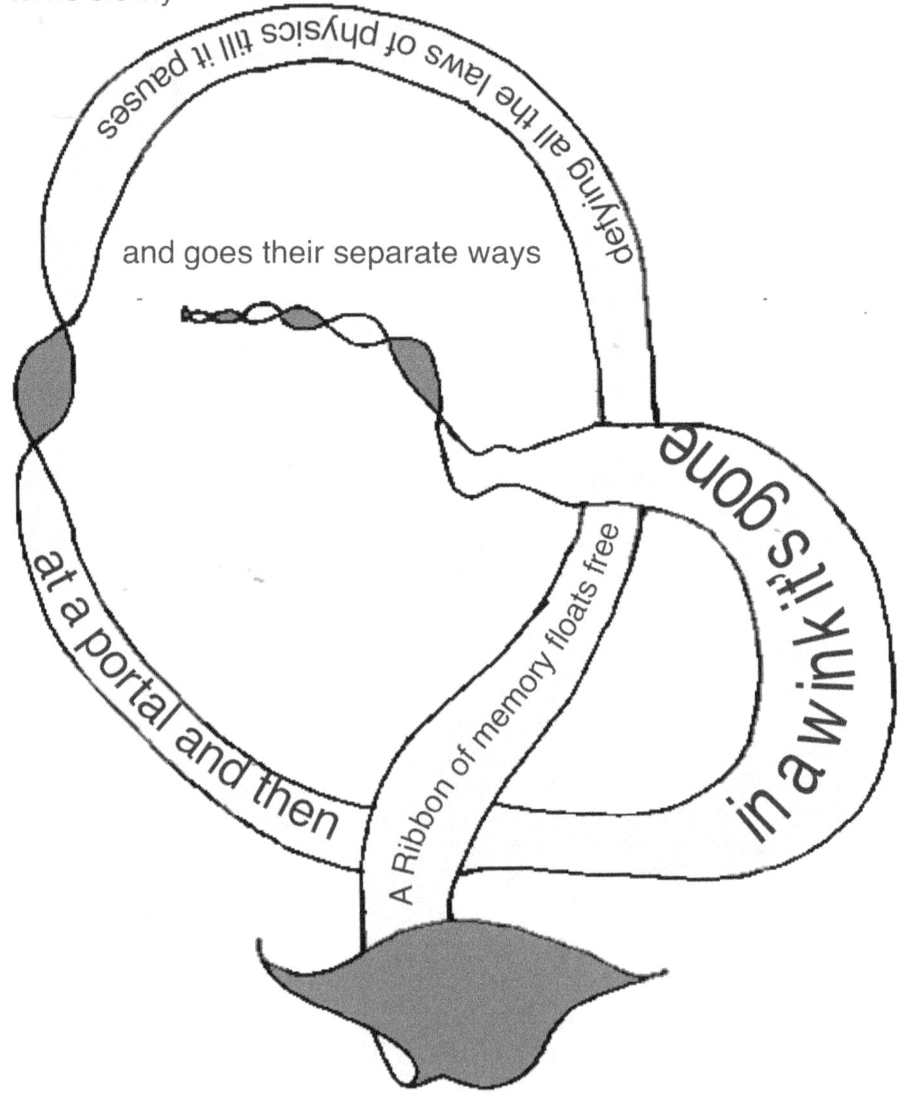

and goes their separate ways

A Ribbon of memory floats free
defying all the laws of physics till it pauses
at a portal and then
in a wink it's gone

RRSPs are wonderful
a tax avoidance gig
till you're 71 then
they bleed you
like a stuck pig

I had a little nest egg
savings for a rainy day
but I thought, the hell with that
and spent it any way

our affairs are in order
our wills are all fine
all we have to do now

is drink up all the wine

Thank you

Thank you very much

Goodbye

God bless

Hope you enjoyed
at least some of
my memories.

Michael.

www.ingramcontent.com/pod-product-compliance
Lightning Source LLC
Chambersburg PA
CBHW061442050726
47593CB00004B/1416

* 9 7 8 1 7 7 7 1 8 6 3 0 2 *